CHINESE

Nita Mehta's
Menus
from around the world

Nita Mehta
B.Sc. (Home Science), M.Sc. (Food and Nutrition), Gold Medalist

SNAB
Publishers Pvt. Ltd.

Nita Mehta's

Menus
from around the world

© Copyright 2001-2006 **SNAB** Publishers Pvt Ltd

4th Print 2006
ISBN   81-7869-003-9

Food Styling and Photography: **SNAB**

Layout and laser typesetting :

National Information
Technology Academy
3A/3, Asaf Ali Road
N.I.T.A. New Delhi-110002
☎ 23252948

Distributed by :

THE VARIETY BOOK DEPOT
A.V.G. Bhavan, M 3 Con Circus,
New Delhi - 110 001
Tel : 23417175, 23412567; Fax : 23415335
Email: varietybookdepot@rediffmail.com

Published by :

Publishers Pvt. Ltd.
3A/3 Asaf Ali Road,
New Delhi - 110002
Tel: 23252948, 23250091
Telefax:91-11-23250091

Editorial and Marketing office:
E-159, Greater Kailash-II, N.Delhi-48
Fax: 91-11-29225218, 23250091
Tel: 91-11-29214011, 29218727, 29218574, 29229558
E-Mail: nitamehta@email.com
nitamehta@nitamehta.com
*Website:*http://www.nitamehta.com
Website: http://www.snabindia.com

Printed by :

BRIJBASI ART PRESS LTD.

Rs. 89/-

With love and affection for
Tanya and Anurag
my loving daughter in law & son

About the Book

*A*re you bored of the usual dinners? Here is help to plan an exciting dinner, very different from the routine. Choose a **complete Italian, Thai, Mexican, Chinese, Indian or an English dinner from the ready-to-use menus offered here.** The menus are well balanced to turn out a perfect meal. Every menu starts with a delicious yet simple to cook starter, followed by a main and a side dish. The meal is rounded off with a splendid dessert. The staple cereal, whether it is a special rice preparation such as risotto or garlic bread, is also included. I have balanced the menus in such a way that the time taken in preparing the meal is not much.

Each recipe has been tried and tested to perfection. So, overcome your fears and gain confidence while preparing these international cuisines. I am sure you will not only love cooking these dishes for your family and friends but also enjoy the appreciation!

Enjoy!

Contents

ITALIAN (Menu 2) 35

T H A I (Menu) 46

ENGLISH (Menu) 56

CHINESE (Menu 1)　65

CHINESE (Menu 2)　80

A QUICK INDIAN DINNER　91

THAI

me**X**ican

Menu

Picture on page 70-71

Southern Belle   (Mocktail)

Nacho Chips with Salsa   (Starter)

Chimichangas (chee-mee-chan-gahs)   (Main Dish)

Mexican Green Rice with Beans   (Side Dish)

Eggless Chocolate Mousse   (Dessert)

Southern Belle

A refreshing blend of mint leaves, fresh lime and ginger ale.

.Picture on page 70-71   *Serves 4*

4 tbsp ginger ale (ready made)
4 tbsp lemon juice (juice of 2 big lemons)
10 tbsp powdered sugar, a pinch of salt
2 tbsp chopped mint leaves
2 bottles chilled soda water
lots of ice cubes

1. In a pan, mix ginger ale, lemon juice, sugar, salt and mint leaves. Mix well to dissolve the sugar. Keep in the refrigerator till serving time.
2. At serving time, put 3-4 ice cubes in each glass.
3. To the ginger-lemon mixture, add some ice cubes and mix well to mix the settled sugar. Add cold soda water and mix quickly.
4. Put in glasses with ice and serve immediately.

Nachos with Salsa

These can be made 5-6 days in advance & stored in an air tight container.
These can also be topped with cheese and grilled in the oven till cheese melts.

Picture on page 70-71   *Serves 4-5*

3/4 cup maize flour (makai ka atta), ½ cup maida (plain flour)
½ tbsp oil, 3/4 tsp salt, ¼ tsp ajwain (carom seeds)
¼ cup warm water to knead

SALSA
5 tomatoes - roasted, 1 tbsp oil
2 onions - chopped finely, 2 green chillies - chopped, 2 tbsp chopped coriander
1 tsp vinegar, ½ tsp salt and ¼ tsp pepper, or to taste

1. Sift both flours and salt together. Add oil and ajwain. Mix well.
2. Knead to a stiff dough (like that for puris) with about ¼ cup warm water. Knead well till smooth and cover and keep aside for 30 minutes.
3. After 30 minutes, knead the dough again.

4. Make small marble sized balls. Roll out into thin chappatis, as thin as you can on a floured board. If the edges break while rolling, do not bother. Roll out thinly into a big round like a chappati. Prick the chappati with a fork all over so that the chips do not puff up on frying.
5. Cut the chappati into 4 pieces so as to get 4 triangles. Cut each triangle further into 2 pieces to get 8 triangular pieces. Make chips similarly with the left over dough.
6. Deep fry 8-10 pieces on medium flame till they turn golden brown in colour. Do not make them dark in colour. Remove from oil on paper napkins to absorb excess oil.
7. Fry all chips. Transfer to a clean dry pan. Sprinkle 1 tbsp maida on them. Gently toss to coat maida on the chips to absorb any excess oil.
8. To prepare salsa, pierce a tomato with a fork. Hold it over the naked flame to roast it till the skin turns blackish and charred. Roast all the tomatoes like this. Cool and peel. Chop 2 tomatoes and puree the other 3 tomatoes. Heat oil and saute onion and green chillies till onion turns soft. Add all other ingredients and cook for just 1 minute. Do not cook further. Remove from fire. Keep aside. Serve with nacho chips.

Chimichangas (pronounced as chee-mee-chan-gahs)

Picture on page 70-71   *Serves 4-5*

7 flour tortillas (8" in diameter), page 18
guacamole, page 19, optional as an accompaniment

FILLING
refried beans, page 20
2-3 cubes (60 gm) cheddar cheese - grated

SALAD
3-4 lettuce leaves - shredded
1 green onion - chopped till the greens, 1 tomato - chopped
50 gm cottage cheese (paneer) - cut into ¼" cubes
1 green chilli - chopped, salt to taste

TOPPING
sour cream, page 19, salsa, page 14
2-3 tbsp chopped spring onion greens or shredded lettuce or chopped capsicum

1. Make tortillas as given on page 18.
2. Make refried beans as given on page 20.
3. Make salsa as given on page 14 and sour cream as given on page 19.
4. Mix all ingredients of the salad filling in a bowl and add salt to taste.
5. To assemble the chimichangas, spread a tortillas on a flat surface. Put 2 tbsp beans at room temperature in the centre and spread in the centre portion. Sprinkle some grated cheese and then some salad filling on top.
6. Fold in 1" from the right and left sides and holding on, fold the top part to cover the filling. Roll on to get a rectangular parcel, making sure that all the filling is enclosed.
7. Repeat for the remaining tortillas, beans, cheese and filling. Cover all with a cling film and keep aside till serving time.
8. Heat some oil in a large frying pan. Reduce heat and put the chimichangas, folded side down first. Cook on both sides until crisp and golden. Drain on absorbent paper. Keep in a serving plate.
9. Spoon some sour cream on the top of each chimichanga and drizzle salsa on it. Sprinkle chopped greens on top and serve immediately.

Flour Tortillas

Makes 7 tortillas

1½ teacup maida (plain flour)
1 tsp baking powder
½ tsp salt
warm water to knead

1. Sift maida with baking powder and salt. Add warm water very gradually to get a crumbly dough. Knead with wet hands till smooth and elastic.

2. Make 7 equal balls. Cover with a plastic wrap or a cling film or a damp cloth and keep aside for 15 minutes.

3. Roll out each ball using a little maida till you get a very thin round of about 8-9" diameter.

4. Heat a tawa (griddle). Cook lightly on one side for about a minute and then turn. Reduce heat and cook the other side also for a minute till light brown specs appear. Wrap in an aluminium foil and keep aside in a casserole. Make all tortillas similarly.

Sour Cream

Picture on page 70-71

½ cup (100 gm) fresh cream - chilled, 1 cup thick curd - hung for 1 hour
1 tsp lemon juice, ¼ tsp salt, or to taste

1. Beat chilled cream until it turns thick and it can stand in soft peaks.
2. Whip curd till smooth. Gently mix cream with the whipped curd. Add salt & lemon juice. Mix lightly. Keep in the refrigerator till serving time.

Guacamole

Picture on page 70-71

1 **ripe, soft** avocados (a hard, under-ripe avocado is bitter)
juice of ½ lemon (1 tbsp), 1 green chilli - chopped, ¼ tsp salt, or to taste
½ onion - chopped finely, 1 tomato - blanched, peeled & chopped finely

1. Cut the ripe avocado in half. Remove the stone. Scoop out the pulp with a spoon but do not go too near the peel because the portion near the peel is generally bitter. Mash pulp with a fork. Add the remaining ingredients. Mash with the back of a fork. Serve at room temperature.

Refried Beans

Refried beans are not literally refried. 'Re' in Spanish means very or thorough.

Picture on page 70-71   *Serves 4-5*

1 cup small red kidney beans (Jammu waale rajmah)
1 large tomato - chopped, 3-4 flakes garlic - chopped, 1 green chilli - chopped
1 large onion - chopped, ½ tsp red chilli powder
2 tbsp butter, 1 tbsp oil, 1¼ tsp salt, or to taste

1. Wash the beans and soak in water overnight in a pressure cooker. Next day, drain. Add 3½ cups fresh water.
2. Add the tomato, garlic, green chilli and half onion. Keep on fire to give 3 whistles. Reduce heat and cook further for 35-40 minutes. Remove from fire. After the pressure drops, mash the beans with a potato masher to a coarse paste. Keep aside.
3. Heat the oil and butter. Fry the remaining half onion till soft.
4. Add beans, chilli powder and salt. Boil and cook on medium heat for 12-15 min till a thick paste is ready. Mash the beans more while cooking.

Mexican Green Rice with Beans

Rice is slowly toasted in oil to give flavour and every grain comes out separate and fluffy.

Picture on page 70-71   *Serves 4*

1 cup long grained basmati rice - washed & put in a strainer for 30 minutes
4 tbsp oil
1 seasoning or stock cube dissolved in 2 cups warm water
¼ tsp red chilli powder, ½ tsp salt, or to taste
1 tomato - put in boiling water and peeled (blanched) & chopped
a drop of green colour, optional

VERY FINELY CHOPPED (MINCED) OR GROUND TO A ROUGH PASTE
1 onion - chopped
3-4 flakes garlic
1 small capsicum - chopped
3 tbsp chopped coriander

1. Wash rice several times. Strain the rice and let the wet rice be in the strainer for about 30 minutes. (If the rice is soaked it gets too soft and breaks when it is toasted in the oil).

2. Put onion, garlic, capsicum and coriander in a small spice grinder and churn for just 2-3 seconds to mince the ingredients or very finely chop everything. Do not grind them to a smooth paste. Heat 1 tbsp oil in a small pan and stir fry this green paste for 3 minutes on medium heat. Keep aside.

3. Heat 3 tbsp oil in a separate heavy bottomed pan and add the rice. Stir fry on low heat gently for 5-6 minutes till well toasted and light brown in colour.

4. Add the green paste, water with the stock cube, salt and red chilli powder. Add a drop of colour. Let it boil. Reduce heat. Taste the water of the rice to see the salt as the seasoning cube has salt in it. In the absence of the cube add plain water and increase the salt. After the boil, cover tightly and keep on low heat till the water gets absorbed, for 13-15 minutes. Serve hot with refried beans given on page 20.

Eggless Chocolate Mousse

Picture on page 70-71   *Serves 4-5*

2 cups milk, 5 tbsp sugar, 2 tsp gelatine, 1 tbsp cornflour, 3 tbsp cocoa powder
40 gm (1 slab) plain chocolate, 3/4 tsp coffee powder
½ tsp vanilla essence, 3/4 cups (150 gm) cream - whipped till fluffy

1. Mix cocoa and cornflour in ¼ cup milk in a small bowl.
2. Boil the rest of milk with sugar in a heavy bottomed pan.
3. Add cocoa & cornflour paste to the boiling milk, stirring continuously.
4. Add chocolate broken into pieces. Cook on low heat for 3-4 minutes till chocolate dissolves. Add coffee and remove from fire.
5. Put ¼ cup water in a small pan. Add gelatine. Dissolve on low heat.
6. Mix the gelatine solution with the chocolate custard. Chill in the freezer till a little thick, but not set. Beat the thickened chocolate custard.
7. Beat cream and essence till slightly thick and fluffy. Add whipped cream to chocolate mixture. Mix gently. Transfer to a serving dish or pour in individual glasses. Refrigerate till set. Decorate with whipped cream.

ITALIAN

Menu 1

Classic Pizzatini	(Starter)
Macaroni & Corn Soup	(Soup)
Fettuccine Primevera	(Main Dish)
Garlic Bread	(Bread)
Lemon Cheese Cake	(Dessert)

Classic Pizzatini

Serve tiny pizzas with different toppings as a starter.

Serves 6

12 readymade cocktail pizza bases
50 gms mozzarella or pizza cheese - grated

TOMATO SPREAD
1 tbsp oil
4-5 flakes of garlic - crushed to a paste (1 tsp)
1/3 cup ready made tomato puree, 1 tbsp tomato sauce
½ tsp oregano (dried), ¼ tsp salt and 2 pinches pepper, or to taste

ADD ONS
1 tbsp tinned sweet corn kernels or thinly sliced baby corns
1 mushroom - cut into paper thin slices
8-10 spinach leaves, 1 tbsp boiled peas
¼ of a green capsicum - diced (1 tbsp)
salt and freshly ground peppercorns and oregano, to taste

1. To prepare the tomato spread, heat 1 tbsp oil. Reduce heat. Add garlic. Stir and add tomato puree & tomato sauce, salt & pepper. Simmer for 3-4 min on low heat. Add oregano. Cook for 2 minutes till thick.
2. Boil 2 cups water with ½ tsp salt. Add spinach. Boil. Remove from fire after 1 minute. Strain and chop. Add boiled peas to spinach.
3. Spread tomato spread on the pizza bases, leaving the edges clean. Sprinkle some cheese on the tomato spread, reserving some for top.
4. Put corn on 4 bases, mushrooms on the other 4 and blanched spinach and peas on the last 4 bases. Spread capsicum on the mushroom and corn pizzatinis. Sprinkle some salt and pepper. Sprinkle the remaining cheese on all of them. Sprinkle some oregano too.
5. Place the pizzas on the wire rack of a hot oven (220°C). Grill for about 8-10 minutes till the base gets crisp and the cheese melts. To get a crisp pizza, oil the bottom of the base a little before grilling.
6. Serve them all together on a platter without cutting, along with some red chilli flakes & mustard sauce.

Note: To make mustard sauce, mix a little cream with some ready-made English mustard paste to get the saucy consistency. To make chilli flakes, coarsely dry-grind the whole red chillies in a small spice grinder.

Macaroni & Corn Soup

Serves 4

1 tbsp butter, 1 onion - finely chopped, 4 flakes garlic - crushed
1¼ cups cream style corn (tinned)
3-4 tbsp chopped basil or coriander leaves
¼ cup uncooked macaroni (small sized)
2½ tsp salt and ½ tsp pepper, or to taste, 3-4 drops of lemon juice
2-3 tbsp grated cheese, to garnish

1. Heat oil. Stir fry onion and garlic on low heat till onion turns soft.
2. Add the creamed corn. Stir fry for a minute.
3. Add 5 cups water, basil or coriander and macaroni. Cook on medium heat, for about 8-10 minutes, till the macaroni is done.
4. Add salt and pepper to taste. Add lemon juice to taste.
5. Serve in soup bowls, garnished with some grated cheese.

Note: Transfer the left over tinned corn in a stainless steel box or a zip lock bag & store in the freezer compartment of the refrigerator for a month.

Fettuccine Primevera

Fettuccine, a flat ribbon pasta, is pronounced as fetu-chee-nee. Vegetables are delightfully combined with this pasta to create this dish. Any other pasta like penne or spiral pasta may be substituted for fettuccine.

Picture on cover   *Serves 4*

200 gm Fettuccine (flat ribbon pasta) - boiled (about 4 cups)
5 tbsp olive oil or butter
6-8 flakes garlic - crushed
75 gm mushrooms - cut into thin slices (1 cup)
1 spring onion - cut diagonally into slices, including the greens
2 red or green or yellow capsicum - cut into four and then cut widthwise into thin
pieces, 6-8 baby corns - cut into diagonal slices of about ¼" thickness
1 tsp maida (plain flour), ½ cup milk
1 cup cream
150 gm cheese, preferably mozzarella - grated (1½ cups)
1 tsp red chilli flakes, 1 tsp oregano
1 tsp salt & ½ tsp freshly ground pepper, or to taste

1. Boil 8 cups of water with 2 tsp salt. When the water starts to boil, add the fettuccine to the pan. Stir well. Boil for about 4-5 minutes till done. Strain. Add fresh water to refresh the pasta and strain again. Sprinkle 1 tbsp oil on the pasta. Keep aside.
2. Heat olive oil or butter in a non stick pan or a kadhai. Reduce heat.
3. Add garlic. Stir for a few seconds. Add mushroom slices. Cook for 2 minutes on high flame.
4. Add the white of spring onion and baby corns and stir fry for 2 minutes.
5. Reduce heat. Add maida. Stir for 30 seconds. Add ½ cup milk, stirring continuously on low heat till the sauce starts to boil. Add salt, pepper and red chilli flakes.
6. Add capsicum and spring onion greens.
7. Keeping the flame low, add the cream. Bring to a boil on low heat.
8. Add fettuccine to the hot sauce.
9. Sprinkle cheese. Remove from fire. Mix well with 2 spoons.
10. Serve immediately. If you want to serve later, always remember to cover the pasta nicely with a cling film as the edges of the pasta tend to turn hard if not covered.

CHINESE

Garlic Bread

Serves 4

a small French bread - cut into slices of 3/4" thickness, about 12 -15 slices
2-3 tbsp olive oil
3-4 flakes garlic - chopped & crushed

1. Mix crushed garlic with olive oil.
2. Spoon ¼ tsp of this flavoured oil on each slice and spread it on the slice with the back of the spoon. Keep aside till serving time.
3. At the time of serving, bake the bread slices in a pre-heated oven at 200°C /360°F for 8 minutes till each is lightly toasted and crisp.

Eggless Lemon Cheese Cake

Picture on cover   *Serves 4-5*

250 gm (1¼ cups) fresh cream, ½ tin (3/4 cup) condensed milk - cold
¼ cup lemon juice (juice of 4 lemons), a pinch or a few drops yellow colour
2 tsp gelatine

BASE

1 packet (10) good day biscuits, 4 tbsp (50 gm) melted butter

1. Keep the cream in a bowl and chill for 10 minutes in the freezer.
2. To prepare the base, preheat oven to 180°C. Break good day biscuits into pieces and put in a polythene. Crush to a coarse powder with a belan (rolling pin). Do not make them too fine. Put them in a bowl.
3. Melt butter. Add 4 tbsp melted butter to the biscuit crumbs. Mix well.
4. Spread crumbs in a small loose bottomed pie dish or a serving dish, (a small round borosil dish in fine). Press well. Bake at 180°C for 10 minutes. Remove from oven and cool.

5. Empty ½ tin of cold condensed milk (keep the condensed milk in the fridge) into a bowl. Add lemon juice and beat well. The condensed milk turns thick on whipping. Keep in the fridge.

6. Beat chilled cream in the chilled bowl with an electric egg beater (hand mixer) till soft peaks are formed. After **soft** peaks are ready, beat gently with a **spoon** till **firm** peaks are formed. Beat carefully in a cool place or over ice, taking care not to beat vigorously. The cream should remain smooth and not turn buttery or granular. Put about ½ cup cream in an icing bag for decoration and keep in the fridge.

7. Add half thickened condensed milk to the cream in the bowl. Fold condensed milk gently into the cream to mix well. Fold in the left over condensed milk too. Add colour to get a nice yellow colour. Keep aside.

8. Put ¼ cup water in a small pan. Sprinkle gelatine on it. After 3-4 minutes keep gelatine on low heat, stirring continuously till it dissolves.

9. Add the gelatine solution in very small amounts to the cream mixture, mixing it well into the cream immediately with the other hand.

10. Pour the cream mix over the cooled biscuit base in the dish. Keep in the fridge for atleast 3 hours. Decorate with icing & serve cold.

ITALIAN

Menu 2

Picture on page 1

Bruschetta with Tomato Basil	(Starter)
Roasted Bell Pepper & Pasta Salad	(Salad)
Corn Minestrone	(Soup)
Eggplant Parmigiana	(Main Dish)
Tiramisu	(Dessert)

Bruschetta with Tomato Basil

Hot & crisp garlic flavoured bread pieces topped with herbed tomatoes at room temperature.

Picture on page 1   *Makes 15 pieces*

BREAD
a small French bread - cut into slices of 3/4" thickness, about 12 -15 slices
2 tbsp olive oil
2-3 flakes garlic - crushed

TOPPING
(mix together and keep aside for at least 30 minutes)
3 tomatoes - pulp removed and chopped finely
6-8 flakes garlic - chopped very finely
1 tbsp fresh basil leaves - chopped, tender tulsi leaves may be used
½ tsp dried oregano, 2-3 tbsp olive oil
½ tsp salt and ½ tsp freshly ground peppercorns, or to taste

1. For the topping, cut each tomato into 4 pieces and gently remove all the seeds and pulp. Chop the deseeded tomatoes into very small pieces.
2. Mix all the other ingredients of the topping with the chopped tomatoes and keep aside for at least 30 minutes for the tomatoes to absorb the flavours. Keep aside at room temperature till serving time.
3. For the bread, mix 2-3 crushed garlic flakes with 2 tbsp olive oil.
4. Spoon ¼ tsp of this flavoured oil on each slice and spread it on the slice with the back of the spoon. Keep aside till serving time.
5. At the time of serving, bake the bread slices in a pre-heated oven at 200°C (360°F) for 8 minutes till each is lightly toasted and crisp.
6. Put 1 heaped tsp of tomato mixture (at room temperature) on the toasted slice. Serve immediately.

Roasted Peppers & Pasta Salad

Picture on page 1   *Serves 4*

200 gm (2½ cups) pasta - bows or spirals or penne
2 large green peppers (capsicums) or 1 red and 1 green pepper
1 tbsp olive oil or any other cooking oil
2-3 tbsp cream or mayonnaise

ITALIAN DRESSING
2 tbsp olive oil
4 flakes garlic - crushed and chopped
4 large tomatoes - blanched & pureed
1 tbsp tomato puree, 2 tbsp tomato sauce
1 tbsp vinegar
1¼ tsp salt, a pinch of sugar, 1 tsp red chilli flakes
1 tsp oregano
1 spring onion greens - sliced, to garnish

1. Boil 8 cups of water with 2 tsp salt. Add pasta. Cook for 12-15 minutes until tender. Drain. Rinse under cold water. Keep in the strainer for 10 minutes to drain out the water. Transfer to a salad bowl and pour 1 tbsp olive oil and cream or mayonnaise on it. Mix well. Keep aside.

2. Pierce a capsicum with a fork and hold it directly on the gas flame. Roast it on all sides for 1-2 minutes till the outer skin of the capsicum gets slightly blackish & charred and the capsicum turns slightly soft. Cool and lightly brush the chard skin. Wash and chop the roasted capsicums into small pieces. Add to the pasta. Keep aside.

3. To prepare the dressing, place the tomatoes in boiling water and boil for 2-3 minutes. Remove from water and cool. Peel the tomatoes and blend in a blender to a smooth puree. Keep aside.

4. Heat 2 tbsp oil in a pan. Reduce heat and add garlic. Stir and add the blanched and pureed tomatoes. Stir for 2-3 minutes and add the tomato puree, tomato sauce, vinegar, salt, oregano, sugar & chilli flakes. Mix.

5. Add ½ cup water and give one boil. Simmer for 3-4 min till it becomes slightly thick. Check seasoning and remove from heat. Cool slightly and pour over the pasta. Toss gently. Cool. Garnish with spring onions.

Corn Minestrone

Serves 4-6

½ cup cooked corn kernels
3 mushrooms - sliced very finely
2 large tomatoes - blanched, peeled and chopped
1 tbsp butter, 2 tbsp chopped onions
½ cup finely chopped spinach, ¼ cup cucumber - finely chopped
4 cups water, 2 tsp salt, ¼ tsp pepper, or to taste
2-3 tbsp grated cheese, to garnish

1. To blanch the tomatoes, put them in boiling water for 3 minutes. Remove from water. Take out the skin and chop them finely.
2. Heat the butter and fry the onions for 1 minute till soft.
3. Add the corn, mushrooms and salt and cook for 2 to 3 minutes.
4. Add the tomatoes, spinach, cucumber and water. Add pepper. Boil. Simmer for about 15-20 minutes, till well blended. Serve hot in soup bowls garnished with grated cheese.

Eggplant Parmigiana

An Italian favourite!

Picture on page 1   *Serves 10-12*

2 eggplants of oblong round variety (bharte ke baingan)
4 cubes cheddar cheese (Britannia) or 75-100 gm mozzarella cheese
oil for frying

TOMATO SAUCE
½ kg large tomatoes - blended to a puree in a mixer
1 onion - chopped finely
4 flakes garlic - crushed
8-10 basil leaves - finely chopped
1 tsp oregano
½ tsp chilli powder, ½ tsp sugar, 1 tsp salt, or to taste
2 tbsp oil
2 tbsp tomato sauce
2 tbsp thick cream

WHITE SAUCE

2½ tbsp butter, 1 small onion - finely chopped
2½ tbsp plain flour (maida)
3 cups milk
1 tsp salt and ¼ tsp pepper, or to taste
2 tbsp thick cream

1. Cut the eggplants into ¼" thick round slices and spread them out on a plate. Sprinkle 1 tsp salt and rub well to salt both sides of the eggplant. Keep aside for 15 minutes. Rinse in water and pat dry on a clean kitchen towel. Deep fry in oil, turning sides, to make them light brown on both sides.

2. To prepare the white sauce, melt the butter in a heavy bottomed pan or a kadhai. Add onion and stir till it just changes colour. Sprinkle flour and cook on low heat for 1 minute without browning, stirring throughout. Remove from heat and gradually add the milk. Mix until well blended. Return to heat and cook slowly for about 5 minutes on low heat, stirring throughout until the sauce thickens and coats the spoon well. Remove from fire. Add cream, salt and pepper. Mix well.

3. For the tomato sauce, heat 2 tbsp oil and fry the onion for 2-3 minutes till it slightly changes colour. Add the tomatoes, tomato sauce, garlic and basil leaves. Add 1 tsp oregano, ½ tsp chilli powder, ½ tsp sugar and 1 tsp salt. Boil for 10 minutes on low heat till the juice from the tomatoes evaporates and it turns slightly thick. Remove from fire and add cream.
4. To assemble, spread 1/3 of the white sauce in a baking dish.
5. Place ½ of the eggplant slices on it. Sprinkle 1-2 tbsp cheese on it.
6. Spread ½ of the prepared tomato sauce over the eggplants.
7. Make another layer with the remaining eggplants. Sprinkle a little cheese on them.
8. Top with the remaining tomato sauce.
9. Spread the remaining white sauce also. Sprinkle left over cheese. Bake for 10 minutes at 200°C till cheese melts.

Tiramisu

Picture on page 1   *Serves 6-8*

400 gm (2¼ cups) fresh cream - chilled in the fridge
1 kg milk - curdled with lemon juice or sour curd to get chenna (fresh home
made paneer), 1 tsp vanilla essence, 3/4 cup powder sugar
1 tbsp rum or brandy (optional), 2-3 tbsp cocoa to sprinkle

ESPRESSO COFFEE (½ CUP)
¼ cup water, ½ cup milk, 1 tsp coffee, 2 tsp sugar

OTHER INGREDIENTS
3 packs of choco chip biscuits

1. Boil milk. Add lemon juice to curdle milk. Strain the milk through a muslin cloth to get chenna. Tie the chenna in the cloth for ½ hour for all the whey to drain out. Blend the chenna in a mixer till creamy.

2. Chill cream in a mixing bowl in the freezer for 10 minutes. Chill the blades of the egg beater also. Whip the cream with sugar, essence and

brandy till soft peaks form. Beat cream over ice or in a cool room during the hot weather. Now gently beat the cream some more with a tablespoon till firm peaks are formed. Do not over beat. If the cream starts looking granular, immediately stop beating. Gently fold the chenna into the cream. Put cream-chenna mixture in the freezer.

3. To prepare espresso coffee, boil water and milk together. Add sugar. Simmer for a minute. Remove from fire. Add coffee & mix well. Cool.

4. Soak choco chip biscuits in coffee for a second and then arrange at the bottom of a small rectangular borosil dish.

5. Spread ½ of the chenna-cream mixture. Level it gently.

6. Again put a layer of soaked biscuits. To get a thicker layer of biscuits, arrange another layer of soaked biscuits on the first layer so as to double the biscuit layer.

7. Spread the remaining cream mixture. Chill in the freezer for 10 minutes.

8. Sift 2 tbsp cocoa through a fine strainer over the dessert. Decorate with cherries or strawberries. Cover with a cling film and keep in the refrigerator (not the freezer) for atleast 3-4 hours till well set. Cut into squares to serve.

THAI
Menu

Picture on page 10-11

Baby Corn & Capsicum Satay
with Peanut Sauce   (Starter)

Tom Yum Soup   (Soup)

Vegetables in Red Curry   (Main Dish)

Stir Fried Mushrooms with Cashewnuts (Side Dish)

Noodles with Bean Sprouts OR Steamed Rice

Tapioca Pearl Pudding   (Dessert)

Baby Corn & Capsicum Satay

with Peanut Sauce

Picture on page 10-11   *Makes 6 Skewers*

12 baby corns, small sized - put in boiling water for 3 minutes and wipe dry
1 green capsicum - cut into 1" cubes
6 cherry tomatoes or 1 large, firm tomato, cut into 8 pieces and pulp removed

MARINADE

½ tsp salt, ¼-½ tsp red chilli powder, 2 tsp brown sugar or gur, 2 tsp oil
2 tbsp coconut milk, 1 tsp lemon juice
½ tsp soya sauce, 8-10 flakes garlic - crushed to a paste
½ tsp jeera powder (ground cumin), ½ tsp dhania powder

PEANUT SAUCE

¼ cup roasted salted peanuts, ½ tsp salt, 1 tbsp oil, 4-6 flakes garlic - crushed
½ tsp red chilli powder, ½-1 tsp sugar, 1½ tsp lemon juice, 1 tsp soya sauce
1 cup coconut milk, fresh or ready made

1. To take out coconut milk, grate a coconut and add 1½ cups hot water to it. Keep aside for 15 minutes. Blend in a strainer and squeeze through a muslin cloth to get fresh coconut milk. You may use 1 cup desiccated coconut mixed with 1 cup hot water and get milk the same way if fresh coconut is not available.

2. Mix all ingredients of the marinade together. Add blanched baby corns, capsicum & tomatoes. Keep covered for ½ hour or till serving time.

3. Thread marinated vegetables onto oiled wooden skewers. Leave behind the marinade. Cook in a preheated grill at 180°C for 7-8 min.

4. To make peanut sauce, grind peanuts with the salt to a rough powder.

5. Heat 1 tbsp oil in a heavy bottomed small pan or kadhai. Add crushed garlic. Saute till it starts to change colour. Reduce heat. Add ½ tsp red chilli powder. Add only ½ cup coconut milk. Boil, stirring. Cook on low heat for 3 minutes, stirring constantly. Stir in the crushed peanuts, ½ tsp sugar, 1½ tsp lemon juice, 1 tsp soya sauce and the remaining ½ cup coconut milk. Boil. Simmer gently for 5 minutes, stirring occasionally to prevent it sticking to the pan. Transfer to a bowl and serve with the prepared satay.

Tom Yum Soup

A clear lemon flavoured soup with paper thin slices of vegetables.

Picture on page 10-11   *Serves 4*

STOCK
5 cups water, 1" piece ginger - sliced
2 tbsp chopped coriander leaves, 3-4 kaffir lime leaves
2 stalks lemon grass, 1 seasoning or stock cube, 2 fresh or dry red chillies

OTHER INGREDIENTS
3-4 mushrooms and 1 small carrot - cut into paper thin diagonal slices
¼ tsp red chilli powder, juice of 1 lemon, ¼ tsp salt, or to taste

1. To prepare the stock, boil all the ingredients together. After the boil, keep covered on low heat for 15 minutes. Strain.
2. Heat 1 tbsp oil in a pan. Add mushrooms and carrots. Saute for 2 minutes on medium flame. Reduce heat. Add red chilli powder and stir for 2-3 seconds. Add the stock into the vegetables. Add lemon juice and salt. Simmer for 4-5 minutes. Serve hot.

Vegetables in Red Curry

Picture on page 10-11   *Serves 4-6*

RED CURRY PASTE

4 **Kashmiri** dry, red chillies - soaked in ½ cup warm water for 10 minutes
½ onion - chopped, 8-10 flakes garlic - peeled, 1½" piece ginger - sliced
1 stalk lemon grass (use only the lower part) or rind of 1 lemon
1½ tsp coriander seeds (dhania saboot)
1 tsp cumin (jeera)
6 peppercorns (saboot kali mirch), 1 tsp salt, 1 tbsp vinegar

VEGETABLES

1 small carrot - peeled and cut into fours lengthwise and then into 1" pieces
4 french beans - threaded and cut into 1" length
6-8 baby corns - cut lengthwise into 2 pieces
3 small brinjals - peeled and diced into ½" pieces (small)
½ small broccoli or ½ of a small cauliflower - cut into medium florets (1 cup)
¼ cup chopped bamboo shoots (optional)

OTHER INGREDIENTS

3 cups coconut milk mixed with 1 tbsp cornflour, ½ tsp soya sauce
15 basil leaves - chopped or coriander leaves
1 tbsp oil, salt to taste, ½ tsp brown sugar

1. Grind all the ingredients of the red curry paste along with the water in which the chillies were soaked, to a very fine paste.
2. Extract 2 cups coconut milk by soaking grated coconut in 1 cup of hot water. Blend and then strain. Keep milk aside. Add more hot water to the left over coconut and blend to get 3 cups of coconut milk in all.
3. Heat the oil, add the red curry paste. Fry for a 2 minutes on low heat.
4. Add ¼ cup of coconut milk. Add vegetables and cook for 2-3 minutes.
5. Add the rest of the coconut milk, soya sauce and chopped basil leaves.
6. Cover & simmer on low heat for 5-7 minutes till vegetables turn tender.
7. Add salt and sugar to taste. Boil for 1 to 2 minutes. Serve hot.

Note: Red curry paste can be made extra and stored in an airtight container, for upto 1 month. Alternatively, freeze upto 3 months. To obtain a bright red curry paste, use dry, broad & big Kashmiri chillies as far as possible and not the usual thin long ones.

Stir Fried Mushrooms with Cashewnuts

Picture on page 10-11   *Serves 4*

200 gms mushrooms - each cut into 2 pieces
¼-½ cup freshly roasted or fried cashewnuts
1 large green or ½ green and ½ red capsicum - cut into 3/4" squares
2 spring onions - cut bulb into 4 pieces and green into 1" long pieces
3 tbsp oil, 1 tbsp chopped & lightly crushed garlic, 1 tbsp finely chopped ginger
½ tsp salt & ¼ tsp peppercorns - crushed
½ tsp sugar, 1 tbsp vinegar, ½ tsp soya sauce
4 fresh red chillies - slit lengthwise, optional

1. Heat 3 tbsp oil in a pan or kadhai. Add white part of onion till onion turns light brown. Add garlic and ginger. Stir.
2. Add mushrooms, salt and pepper. Stir fry on high flame, keeping them spaced apart, for 4-5 minutes till light brown and the water evaporates, and they turn dry. Reduce heat. Add sugar, vinegar and soya sauce.
3. Add green & red capsicums, cashewnuts, greens of spring onion and red chillies. Sprinkle ¼ tsp of salt. Saute for 1-2 minutes. Serve hot.

Noodles with Bean Sprouts

Moong bean sprouts with 1-1½" long shoots should be used.

Picture on page 10-11   *Serves 4-5*

7-8 cups boiled (400 gms) noodles, preferably, flat rice noodles
2 cups bean sprouts with long shoots
1 large carrot - cut into thin match sticks or juliennes
1 large capsicum - cut into thin long pieces or juliennes
10 -12 garlic flakes - crushed (1½ tbsp)
2 spring onions - chop the white part finely and cut the greens into 1" pieces
1½ tsp sugar, 2½ tsp salt
4 tbsp vinegar or tamarind juice
4 tbsp roasted peanuts - coarsely ground
5 tbsp oil

RED CHILLI PASTE

4-5 dry red chillies soaked in ¼ cup hot water for 15 minutes and ground to a paste in a small spice grinder to get 5-6 tsp of red chilli paste. Use as required and store the rest in the refrigerator.

1. Soak rice noodles in warm water for 10-12 minutes. Rinse in cold water. Drain and keep aside. There is no need to boil the rice noodles but if you are using the ordinary noodles put them in salted boiling water. Keep them boiling for just 2 minutes. Remove from fire and strain. Add fresh water and strain again. Strain using several changes of water. Keep aside in the strainer for all the water to drain out.

2. To cut match sticks of carrots, peel and cut the carrot into 2" pieces. Cut each piece lengthwise into very thin slices. Cut each slice into very thin long pieces using the tip of the knife. Keep aside.

3. Wash sprouts in several changes of water. Leave in the strainer.

4. Heat 5 tbsp oil in a non stick wok or pan. Reduce heat. Add garlic. Fry for 1 minute. Reduce heat. Add only 3-4 tsp of red chilli paste. Fry for about 1-2 minutes till it leaves oil.

5. Add bean sprouts and white of spring onions. Fry for 1 minute.

6. Add capsicum, carrots and spring onion greens. Mix. Stir fry for 1 minute. Reduce heat.

7. Add noodles. Do not mix. Add 2½ tsp salt, 1½ tsp sugar, 4 tbsp vinegar and 4 tbsp peanuts. Increase heat and mix well using 2 spoons. Serve hot sprinkled with some roasted & crushed peanuts.

Tapioca Pearl Pudding

Picture on page 10-11   *Serves 4-6*

This pudding is made from Tapioca pearls similar to saboodana & coconut milk. Adjust sweetness to your liking. It is served with some crushed ice added to it, accompanied with chilled fresh fruits.

3/4 cup tapioca pearls or saboodana, 1½ cups coconut milk
1½ cups water, 7½ tbsp sugar or jaggery (gur), a pinch of salt
finely shredded lemon-rind of ½ lemon (optional) used for garnishing

1. Soak saboodana in warm water for 1-2 hours, till they swell up. Drain.
2. Put water to boil in a saucepan. Add sugar/gur and salt.
3. When sugar has dissolved, add saboodana and coconut milk. Boil.
4. Simmer for 5 minutes. Transfer to a serving bowl. Keep in the fridge.
5. To serve, add crushed ice in the bowl of dessert which thins it a little. Garnish with lemon rind.
6. Serve delicately carved and chilled fruits with it.

ENGLISH

Menu

Cheese Surprise	(Starter)
Cream of Almond Soup	(Soup)
Stuffed Cheese Steak with Tomato Relish	(Main Dish)
Light Sesame Vegetables	(Side Dish)
A Bread Basket with Butter	(Bread)
Mocha Souffle	(Dessert)

Cheese Surprise

Serves 4-6

4 slices of wheat bread or white bread, some butter to spread
4 cheese slices
½ onion - chopped very finely
¼ capsicum - chopped very finely
½ tomato - chopped very finely without pulp

1. Trim the edges of the slices. Butter both sides of the bread lightly.
2. Place a cheese slice on each piece of bread.
3. Sprinkle some very finely chopped onion, tomato and capsicum. Keep aside.
4. At the time of serving place the bread slice on a non stick tawa. Cover the tawa with a large lid. Toast the squares for 5 minutes on low heat till the bread gets toasted on the bottom.
5. Cut into four pieces with a pizza cutter or a knife. Serve hot.

Cream of Almond Soup

An economical, yet delicious, almond soup.

Serves 4

20 almonds - blanched (put in hot water and skinned) & chopped
½ of a small cauliflower - remove stalk & break into tiny florets (1½ cups)
1 tbsp oil / melted butter
3 cups water
1½ cups milk
1 tsp salt & ½ tsp pepper, or to taste

GARNISHING

some fresh dhania leaves (coriander) - chopped
a few blanched & finely chopped almonds
4-5 saboot kali mirch (peppercorns) - crushed

1. In a pressure cooker heat 1 tbsp oil & saute the tiny florets of cauliflower for 3-4 minutes on low flame.
2. Add 3 cups water & give 3-4 whistles. Remove from fire.
3. In a liquidiser or a small grinder, put blanched (skin removed by soaking in hot water) & chopped almonds with ½ cup milk and blend them well to a smooth thin paste. Remove the almond milk from the grinder and add 1 more cup of milk to the almond paste. Keep aside.
4. When the cooker cools down, put the cauliflower along with all the water in the mixer and churn till it turns into a smooth puree.
5. Mix cauliflower puree & almond milk together. Boil.
6. Add salt & pepper to taste. Garnish with coriander leaves, some crushed peppercorns & a few almonds if desired. Serve hot.

Stuffed Cheese Steaks

Picture on back cover   *Serves 4*

400 gm cottage cheese (paneer) - cut into 3/4" thick squares or rounds of 2"

FILLING
½ cube cheese - grated finely (2 tbsp)
½ tbsp butter, 1 tbsp grated onion (½ onion)
6-7 french beans - cut into paper thin slices, ¼ cup finely grated carrot
¼ tsp salt, ¼ tsp oregano, a pinch of pepper, or to taste

BATTER
3 tbsp plain flour (maida), ¼ cup plus 1 tbsp milk
2 pinches of turmeric (haldi), ¼ tsp salt, ¼ tsp red chilli powder
2 tbsp very finely grated cheese

TOMATO RELISH
5 tomatoes - roasted, 2 onion - chopped finely
2 green chillies - chopped, 2 tbsp chopped coriander
1 tbsp oil, 1 tsp vinegar, ½ tsp salt and ¼ tsp pepper, or to taste

1. Cut cottage cheese into thick, big round pieces. Divide each piece into 2 thinner pieces. Sprinkle salt & pepper on both sides.
2. For the filling, heat butter. Reduce heat. Add 1 tbsp grated onion. Stir fry for 2 minutes. Add beans. Cook covered for 3 minutes on low heat till soft. Add carrots, salt, pepper, oregano, grated cheese and stir for 1 minute. Remove from fire and keep aside to cool.
3. Take a piece of paneer. Spread 1 tsp of the filling on it. Press another piece of paneer on it. Turn and press the other side also. Keep aside.
4. For the batter, mix all ingredients of the batter together.
5. To prepare the tomato relish, pierce a tomato with a fork and hold it over the naked flame to roast it till the skin turns blackish and charred. Roast all the tomatoes like this. Cool and peel. Chop 2 tomatoes and puree the other 3 tomatoes. Heat oil and saute onion and green chillies till onion turns soft. Add all other ingredients and cook for 2-3 minutes.
6. At serving time heat ½ tbsp butter in a pan on medium heat. Dip the stuffed steak in the prepared batter to coat all sides and put in the pan. Cook 4 pieces at a time. Reduce heat after 2 minutes when the edges start changing colour. Turn the side gently with a knife or a flat spoon. Cook till browned on both sides. Serve hot with tomato relish.

Light Sesame Vegetables

Picture on back cover   *Serves 4-6*

250 gm broccoli or cauliflower - cut into small florets
100 gm baby corns - cut diagonally into slices
200 gms mushrooms (small) - keep them whole, only trim the stem
1 carrot - peeled and sliced diagonally
2 tbsp butter or olive oil, 2-3 flakes garlic - crushed, 2 tbsp til (sesame seeds)
1 tomato - very finely chopped, 1 tsp salt, ½ tsp pepper, 1 tbsp lemon juice,

1. Boil 4-5 cups of water with 2 tsp salt in a pan. Add the vegetables. After the boil returns, keep boiling for ½ minute only. Strain. Refresh in cold water. Keep aside.

2. Heat 2 tbsp butter or oil in a pan. Reduce heat. Add garlic. Stir and add the sesame seeds. Stir for a few seconds on low heat.

3. Add the blanched vegetables. Cook for 3-4 minutes on medium flame till well coated in butter. Add tomato, salt and pepper. Stir and add lemon juice. Remove from fire. Serve hot.

Crunchy Mocha Souffle

Serves 6-8

1 packet chocolate chip biscuits
125 gm (slightly less than 1 cup) sugar
1½ cups water, 2 tsp nescafe instant coffee
2½ tsp gelatine
350 gm (2 cups) cream
1 tsp vanilla essence

1. Transfer the cream to a pan and keep in the freezer for 10 minutes.
2. Boil water. Remove from fire. Add coffee. Keep the black coffee aside.
3. Heat sugar in a big, heavy bottomed kadhai or pan on slow fire. Keep stirring continuously till sugar melts.
4. Continue cooking, till sugar turns golden brown. Remove from fire.
5. Carefully add the prepared hot black coffee into the caramel syrup. Simmer for 2-3 minutes on low heat, stirring continuously, till caramel dissolves. Remove from fire. Cool to room temperature.

6. Beat chilled cream till it gets fluffy and attains a thick pouring consistency. Keep in the fridge.

7. Dissolve gelatine in 4 tbsp water. Heat on very low flame till is completely dissolved. Do not boil.

8. Add the gelatine solution to the coffee-caramel syrup, stirring continuously. Add essence and 1¾ cups cream, leaving aside ¼ cup for decoration.

9. Mix well. Keep ½ cup aside and chill the rest in the freezer till slightly thick (for about 15 minutes).

10. Soak the biscuits for a second in the ½ cup coffee-caramel syrup kept aside and arrange at the bottom of a 2" high serving dish. Cover the base of the dish with soaked biscuits.

11. Pour the thickened cream mixture over the biscuits in the dish. Keep in the fridge till it sets. Keep aside till serving time.

12. Crumble 2-3 chocolate chip biscuits. Mix in some chopped almonds or any nuts. Keep aside.

13. Just 15 minutes before serving, sprinkle the biscuit and nut mixture on top. Keep in the freezer so that it is properly chilled when served.

CHINESE

Menu 2

Toasted Gold Coins with Sesame Seeds	(Starter)
Talumein Soup	(Soup)
Spicy Honey Veggies	(Main Dish)
Cottage Cheese in Hot Garlic Sauce	(Side Dish)
Vegetable Haka Noodles	(Noodles)
Almond Float	(Dessert)

Baby Corn Bullets

If baby corns are unavailable, use mushrooms instead.

Picture on page 30-31   *Serves 4-6*

12 baby corns - keep whole if thin and cut lengthwise in 2 long pieces if thick

BATTER
3 tbsp cornflour, 3 tbsp maida (plain flour)
3/4 tsp salt, ¼ tsp pepper, a pinch of baking powder
½ tsp soya sauce, 2 tsp lemon juice
6-8 flakes garlic - crushed to a paste
3-4 tbsp water

TOPPING
1 tbsp oil, 1 spring onion - finely chopped upto the greens
1 green chilli - chopped, 1 dry red chilli - broken into small bits
3-4 flakes garlic - crushed, ½ tsp soya sauce
a pinch of ajinomoto, salt and pepper to taste

1. If the baby corns are thick, cut them into half lengthwise otherwise keep them whole. Boil 4 cups of water with 1 tsp salt. Add the baby corns. Boil. Keep boiling for 2 minutes. Remove from fire and drain. Wipe dry on a clean kitchen towel. Keep aside.

2. To prepare the batter, mix all ingredients of the batter with 3-4 tbsp water to make a batter of a thick coating consistency. Keep aside for 10 minutes or till serving time.

3. To prepare the topping, heat oil. Reduce heat and add garlic, stir for a few seconds. Add green chilli, red chilli bits, spring onions. Keeping the heat low, add soya sauce, salt, pepper and ajinomoto. Stir for a few seconds and remove from fire.

4. At serving time, dip the baby corns in the prepared batter and deep fry on medium heat in 2-3 batches, till golden brown and crisp. Remove from oil on to paper napkins to absorb the excess oil. Transfer to a serving platter.

5. Heat the topping of onions and sprinkle over the baby corn bullets. Serve with chilli garlic sauce.

Hot & Sour Soup

Picture on page 30-31   *Serves 6*

TOMATO STOCK
6 cups water, 2 big tomatoes

OTHER INGREDIENTS
2 tbsp oil
1 tomato - cut into 4, pulp removed and chopped very finely
½ cup chopped cabbage, ½ cup grated carrot
1 tbsp very finely cut french beans
1-2 tbsp dried, Chinese mushrooms - soaked for ½ hour (optional)
½ tsp ajinomoto (optional), ½ tsp sugar
3 tsp salt, or to taste, 3/4 tsp black pepper powder
1½ tsp chilli sauce, 1½ tbsp vinegar, 1tsp soya sauce
4 tbsp cornflour mixed with ½ cup water
50 gms tofu or paneer - diced (cut into tiny cubes), optional

1. Pressure cook water and tomatoes together to give 2-3 whistles. Strain. Mash the tomatoes well to squeeze out all the liquid. Keep the tomato stock aside.
2. If dried mushrooms are available, soak them in water for ½ hour to soften. Wash in several changes of water to clean them properly. Discard the lower hard portion and break them into small pieces.
3. Heat oil. Add chopped tomato. Stir and mash the tomatoes while cooking them. Cook for 1 minute.
4. Add cabbage, carrot and beans. Drain the mushrooms and add to the vegetables. Stir fry for 1 minute.
5. Add the prepared tomato stock.
6. Add all the other ingredients except cornflour paste. Boil for 2 minutes.
7. Add cornflour paste, stirring continuously. Cook for 2-3 minutes till the soup turns thick.
8. Add diced tofu or paneer. Serve hot, accompanied with green chillies in vinegar.

MEXICAN

méxican

Spinach & Carrot in Garlic Sauce

Picture on page 30-31   *Serves 4*

200 gm spinach (paalak), choose spinach with small leaves
1 carrot

HOT GARLIC SAUCE
12-15 flakes garlic - chopped very finely and crushed lightly
2-3 dried, red chillies - broken into small bits
2 tbsp tomato ketchup
2 tsp vinegar
1 tsp salt, ¼ tsp pepper, or to taste
¼ tsp sugar
1½ tbsp cornflour dissolved in 1 cup water
2 tbsp oil

1. Wash spinach. Discard stems, keeping the leaves whole. Peel the carrot.
2. Boil 3-4 cups water with 1 tsp salt in a pan. Drop the carrot in boiling water. Boil the carrot for 2 minutes. Remove from fire and remove the carrot with a slotted spoon, reserving the hot water. Steam the spinach leaves by keeping them in a metal strainer or a colander over the pan of hot water. Keep on fire and let the water keep boiling for 5 minutes to steam the spinach. Remove from fire. Keep steamed spinach aside.
3. Cut 4-5 grooves or slits in the carrot along the length of the carrot. Then cut the carrot widthwise into slices to get flowers. You can also cut the boiled carrot into diagonal or round slices.
4. To prepare the garlic sauce, heat oil. Remove from fire. Add garlic.
5. Add dried red chilli bits. Stir for a few seconds.
6. Add tomato ketchup and vinegar. Return to fire. Cook on low heat for 2-3 minutes till oil separates.
7. Add carrots. Stir for 1 minute on low heat.
8. Add the cornflour paste, stirring continuously. Add salt, pepper and sugar. Boil. Cook for 2-3 minutes on low heat till it turns thick to a saucy consistency. Mix in the steamed spinach. Serve hot.

Vegetable Manchurian

Picture on page 30-31   *Serves 4*

MANCHURIAN BALLS
1 cup grated cauliflower, ¼ cup grated carrots, ¼ cup grated cabbage
1 slice bread - dipped in water and squeezed well
1 tbsp cornflour, 1 tbsp flour (maida)
¼ tsp ajinomoto, salt and pepper to taste, ½ tsp soya sauce
oil for frying

MANCHURIAN SAUCE
2 tbsp oil
1" piece ginger - crushed to a paste, 5-6 flakes garlic - chopped & lightly
crushed, 2 green chillies - chopped, ½ onion - very finely chopped
1 tsp soya sauce, 1½ tbsp tomato ketchup
2 tsp vinegar, ½ tsp salt, ¼ tsp pepper
1½ tbsp cornflour
1 spring onion greens - chopped finely, to garnish

1. Grate all 3 vegetables. Mix all the other ingredients of the balls, adding only 1 slice of bread first. (More bread may be added if balls fall apart on frying.) Make oval balls. Add 1-2 tbsp milk, if the balls do not bind together easily. Flatten each ball.
2. Deep fry 3-4 pieces at a time on medium flame. Reduce flame after the balls turn very light brown and fry on low heat till the balls get cooked from inside and turn brown. Keep the balls aside.
3. To prepare the manchurian sauce, heat 2 tbsp oil. Reduce heat. Add ginger and garlic. Fry on low flame for 30 seconds.
4. Add green chillies and onions. Cook till onions turn light brown.
5. Reduce heat and add soya sauce, tomato sauce, vinegar, salt and pepper. Cook for 2 minutes.
6. Add 1½ cups of water. Boil. Simmer on low heat for 2-3 minutes.
7. Dissolve cornflour in ½ cup water and add to the above sauce, stirring continuously. Cook till slightly thick and coats the spoon. Keep aside.
8. To serve, boil the sauce. Add the balls to the manchurian sauce and keep on slow fire for 1 minute till the balls are heated through. Serve hot sprinkled with finely chopped spring onion greens.

Vegetable Fried Rice

Picture on page 30-31   *Serves 4*

1½ cups uncooked rice, preferably golden sela rice (parboiled rice)
2 tbsp oil
2 green chillies - chopped finely
2 spring onions - chopped along with the greens
2 flakes garlic - chopped & crushed
¼ cup very finely sliced french beans
1 carrot - finely diced (cut into tiny cubes)
½ big capsicum - diced
1 tsp salt, ½ tsp of each of pepper & ajinomoto
½-1 tsp soya sauce (according to the colour desired)
1 tsp vinegar, optional

1. Clean, wash and soak rice for 10 minutes. Boil 6 cups water with 2 tsp salt. Drain and add rice to boiling water. Cook uncovered till the rice is just done and still firm. Do not overcook. Strain. Keep in the strainer for 10 minutes to let all the water drain out. Fluff up the rice with a fork to let the steam escape and to separate the grains of rice. Spread out the cooked rice on a large tray and keep under the fan to dry out nicely. (This makes it turn a little chewy, as the Chinese like it.)
2. Chop green onions, keeping the chopped green part separate.
3. Heat oil. Reduce heat. Splutter green chillies.
4. Stir fry garlic and the white of onions, leaving the green part.
5. Add beans, then carrots. Stir fry for 1 minute. Add capsicum.
6. Add salt, pepper & ajinomoto.
7. Add rice. Add soya sauce and vinegar.
8. Add the green onions and salt to taste. Stir fry the rice for 2 minutes. Serve hot.

Toffee Apples

Picture on page 30-31   *Serves 4*

2 apples, golden or red variety
¼ cup plain flour (maida), 2 tbsp cornflour, ¼ tsp baking powder

TOFFEE COATING
½ cup sugar, 1½ tbsp oil, ¼ cup water
1 tsp sesame (til) seeds
oil for deep frying

1. To prepare the toffee coating, put ½ cup sugar, 1½ tbsp oil and ¼ cup of water in a heavy bottomed pan or a kadhai & stir on a high flame.
2. When the mixture begins to boil, reduce heat and stir continuously to melt the sugar. Stir the syrup for about 3-4 minutes after the first boil or until it is light golden in colour and feels sticky when felt between the thumb and the fore finger. It forms a thread when the finger is pulled apart.

3. Remove the syrup from heat, add the sesame seeds and mix well. Keep the toffee syrup aside.

4. Mix the plain flour, cornflour and baking powder in a bowl. Add enough water, about ¼ cup to get a smooth, thick batter of a coating consistency. Keep aside.

5. Peel and cut the apples into four pieces. Further cut each piece into two lengthwise, thus getting 8 long pieces from each apple. Remove the seeds.

6. Keep a mixing bowl filled with ice-cubes ready and cover with water.

7. Heat oil for frying. Dip the apple pieces in the batter to coat evenly and deep fry 5-6 pieces together at one time. Remove from oil when they turn golden.

8. Put the fried apples in the toffee syrup and coat evenly. Drain well and dip immediately into the ice-cold water. Keep in chilled water for a few minutes till the toffee coating hardens.

9. Drain thoroughly. Keep aside till serving time.

10. Serve plain or with ice cream, sprinkled with some more sesame seeds.

CHINESE

Menu 1

Picture on page 30-31

Baby Corn Bullets (Starter)

Hot & Sour Soup (Soup)

Spinach & Carrot in Garlic Sauce (Main Dish)

Vegetable Manchurian (Side Dish)

Vegetable Fried Rice (Rice)

Toffee Apples (Dessert)

Toasted Gold Coins
with Sesame Seeds

Serves 4-6

6 bread slices - toasted till crisp and light brown
2 small potatoes - boiled
1 spring onion - chopped finely upto the greens (keep greens separate)
1 carrot - grated coarsely
1 capsicum - chopped finely
½-1 tsp soya sauce, use according to colour desired
salt & pepper to taste
¼ tsp chilli powder
¼ tsp ajinomoto (optional)
1 tbsp white til (sesame seeds)

1. Grate boiled potatoes.
2. Heat 1½ tbsp oil. Add only the white part of spring onions. Cook for a minute, till transparent.
3. Add carrots, capsicum and the green onions. Cook for 1-2 minutes on low flame.
4. Add potatoes, soya sauce, salt, pepper, chilli powder and ajinomoto. Cook for 2-3 minutes. Keep aside.
5. With a cutter or a sharp lid of a bottle, cut out small rounds (about 1½" diameter) of the bread.
6. Spread some potato mixture in a heap on the round piece of toasted bread in the centre leaving ¼" edges of the bread. Press.
7. Sprinkle sesame seeds. Press gently. Keep aside till serving time.
8. At the time of serving, heat in an oven. Serve hot, dotted with chilli-garlic sauce.

Talumein Soup

Serves 4

5 cups water, 2-3 seasoning (stock) cubes, ½ carrot
2-3 cabbage leaves - roughly torn into small bite size pieces, (3/4")
½ cup boiled noodles - broken into shorter lengths, about 3-4"
2 tbsp cornflour dissolved in ¼ cup water, 1 tsp vinegar
½ tsp soya sauce, salt to taste, ½ tsp sugar, ¼ tsp black pepper

1. Boil 5 cups water. Peel and wash carrot. Put it into boiling water. Let it boil for 1 minute. Remove from fire. Take out the carrot from water with a slotted spoon. Refresh the carrot in cold water and then cut into paper thin diagonal slices or into flowers. Keep aside.
2. To the hot water add stock cube, pepper, sugar & soya sauce
3. Add cornflour. Keep on fire. Boil, stirring continuously. Boil for 2 min.
4. Add carrot and cabbage. Add vinegar. Boil for 2-3 minutes. Check if salt is required. (Seasoning cube has salt). Add boiled noodles, remove from fire. Serve hot with 2-3 chopped green chillies in ¼ cup vinegar with ¼ tsp salt and ¼ tsp sugar in it.

Spicy Honey Veggies

Serves 4

1 large carrot
8-10 mushrooms - trim stalks and keep whole
8-9 baby corns - keep whole if small and divide into two lengthwise, if thick
1½ cup cauliflower or broccoli - cut into small, flat florets (¼ of a small flower)
1 onion - cut into 8 pieces and separated
1 capsicum - cut into ½" cubes
3 tbsp cornflour dissolved in ½ cup water with 1 seasoning cube
4 tbsp oil
3-4 dry, red chillies - broken into bits, 15 flakes garlic - crushed
3/4 tsp salt and ¼ tsp pepper, or to taste
a pinch ajinomoto, ¼ tsp red chilli powder
1½ tbsp vinegar, 1 tsp soya sauce
2½ tbsp tomato ketchup
3 tsp red chilli sauce
3-4 tsp honey, according to taste

1. Boil 4 cups water with 1 tsp salt. Peel carrot. Drop the whole carrot, mushroom and baby corns in boiling water. As soon as the boil returns, keep boiling for 1 minute. Remove from fire and strain the vegetables. Refresh veggies in cold water.

2. Cut parboiled carrot into ¼" thick round slices or flowers. To make flowers, make slits or grooves along the length of the boiled carrot, leaving a little space between the slits. Cut the grooved carrot widthwise into slices to get flowers. Cut capsicum into ½" pieces. Cut onion into fours and separate the slices.

3. Dissolve cornflour in ½ cup water. Add seasoning cube & keep aside.

4. Heat oil in a kadhai. Reduce heat. Add broken red chillies and garlic.

5. Stir and add baby corns, carrots, cauliflower, onion and mushrooms. Stir for 2-3 minutes or till veggies are done. Add capsicum. Reduce heat. Add salt & pepper. Add ajinomoto and ¼ tsp red chilli powder.

6. Stir and add chilli sauce, tomato sauce, soya sauce, honey and vinegar. Lower heat and stir for ½ minute.

7. Add the dissolved cornflour and seasoning cube. Cook till the vegetables get done and the sauce coats the veggies.

Cottage Cheese in Hot Garlic Sauce

Picture on page 2   *Serves 4-6*

200 gm cottage cheese (paneer)
2 tbsp cornflour
3 tbsp plain flour (maida)
¼ tsp each of pepper & salt
¼ tsp ajinomoto, optional
4 tbsp water

GARLIC SAUCE

30 flakes garlic - chopped & crushed roughly in a small spice grinder (1½ tbsp)
3 tbsp oil, 2 dry red chillies - broken into bits
1 capsicum - cut into tiny cubes
4 tbsp tomato ketchup, 2 tsp red chilli sauce, ½ tsp pepper, 1 tsp salt
¼ tsp sugar, ¼ tsp ajinomoto (optional), 2 tsp vinegar
1½ cups water
2 tbsp cornflour mixed with ½ cup water

1. To prepare the sauce, peel and grind the garlic to a very rough paste in a small grinder. Keep the mixer on just for 1-2 seconds.
2. Heat oil. Remove from fire. Add garlic and red chilli bits. Stir till garlic starts to change it's colour.
3. Add tomato ketchup, red chilli sauce, pepper & salt. Return to fire and cook for 1 minute on low heat. Add vinegar, sugar and ajinomoto.
4. Add capsicum. Stir for 1-2 seconds to mix.
5. Add water. Bring to a boil and simmer for 2 minutes.
6. Add cornflour paste, stirring all the time. Cook for 2 minutes on low heat. Remove from heat. Keep sauce aside.
7. Cut cottage cheese into 1" cubes.
8. Make a thick coating batter by mixing cornflour, plain flour, salt, pepper and ajinomoto with a little water.
9. Dip paneer pieces & deep fry to a golden colour.

Vegetable Haka Noodles

Picture on page 2   *Serves 4*

CHILLI NOODLES

400 gms haka noodles - boiled & spread in a tray
4 tbsp oil
4-5 dry, whole red chillies - broken into bits
½ tsp chilli flakes or powder, 2 tsp salt
½-1 tsp soya sauce

VEGETABLES

1 capsicum - shredded finely
1 carrot - cut into fine juliennes or match sticks
1 cup shredded cabbage
6-8 flakes garlic - crushed and chopped - optional
2 spring onions or 1 small onion - shredded
2 tbsp bean sprouts - optional
3-4 tbsp dried black mushrooms or finely sliced fresh mushrooms
1 tsp salt & ½ tsp pepper, ½ tsp ajinomoto, 1 tbsp vinegar

1. Heat 4-5 tbsp oil. Remove from fire, add broken red chillies and red chilli flakes or powder.
2. Return to fire & mix in the boiled noodles. Add salt and a little soya sauce. Do not add too much soya sauce. Fry for 2-3 minutes, till the noodles turn a pale brown. Keep the fried noodles aside.
3. To prepare the vegetables, shred all vegetables.
4. Heat 2 tbsp oil.
5. Reduce heat & add garlic. Cook for ½ minute.
6. Add vegetables in sequence of their tenderness - onions, sprouts, mushrooms, capsicum, carrot and cabbage. Add vinegar.
7. Add ajinomoto, salt and pepper. Cook for ½ minute. Slide in the noodles and mix well.

Almond Float

Serves 4

2½ cups milk, ¼ cup sugar
2-3 drops almond essence, 6-7 almonds - cut into very thin long pieces
2 tbsp gelatine, ½ cup water

TO SERVE
½ cup (100 gm) cream mixed with 1 tbsp powdered sugar
some fresh fruits like mangoes, grapes, lychees etc.

1. Boil milk with sugar. Remove from fire. Cool slightly. Add essence.
2. Sprinkle gelatine over ½ cup water kept in a small pan. Keep aside for 5 min. Keep gelatine on low heat and stir continuously till it dissolves.
3. Remove from fire and add the gelatine solution to milk mixture.
4. Transfer to a rectangular dish to get 3/4" thick layer. Sprinkle almonds on top. Keep in the fridge to set. Do not put in the freezer.
5. When ready to serve, cut almond gelatine into diamond shapes. Place fruit in a shallow serving dish and arrange diamond shapes on top. Pour some whipped cream on fruit and serve.

A QUICK INDIAN DINNER

Menu

Poodina Jal Jeera	(Drink)
Kandhari Bhel on Paapri	(Starter)
Quick Paneer Makhani	(Main Dish)
Til Mil Aloo Matar	(Side Dish)
Bread Dahi Bada	(Accompaniment)
Jeere waale Chaawal	(Rice)
Shahi Gulabo Kheer	(Dessert)

Kandhari Bhel on Paapri

Picture on inside back cover   *Serves 4-5*

20 pieces of paapri (ready made paapri for chaat) or golgappas
some fine sev (Bikaneri sev)
½ cup anaar ke dane (fresh pomegranate seeds), preferably red kandhari anaar
2 tbsp finely chopped kheera (cucumber), 1-2 tbsp finely chopped tomato
1 tbsp chopped coriander leaves, 1-2 green chillies - deseeded & chopped
salt and ¼ tsp saboot kaali mirch (peppercorns) - crushed
2 tbsp imli chutney, chaat masala to sprinkle

1. Mix anaar ke daane, kheera, tomato, green chillies and coriander. Add salt and crushed black peppercorns to taste.
2. At serving time, spoon the anaar chaat over the flat side of the paapri or make a hole in the golgappa and fill some inside.
3. Put ½ tsp of imli chutney and sprinkle some namkeen sev on top. Sprinkle chat masala. Serve.

Poodina Jal Jeera

Serves 4

4 cups water
4 tbsp seedless imli (tamarind)
4 tsp fresh lime juice
3 tbsp sugar
1" piece ginger - crushed roughly
¼ cup fresh poodina (mint leaves) - minced
½ tsp bhuna jeera powder (roasted ground cumin)
½ tsp black salt and salt to taste
½ tsp red chilli powder, or to taste

1. Soak imli in 1 cup hot water for about one hour. Mash well and extract juice. Add the remaining 3 cups water.
2. Mix all ingredients to the tamarind water. Mix well.
3. Chill for 2-3 hours in the fridge for the flavours to penetrate.
4. At serving time, strain through a fine sieve. Adjust seasonings.
5. Serve garnished with mint leaves and a lemon slice.

Quick Paneer Makhani

Picture on inside back cover   *Serves 4*

250 gm paneer - cut into 1" cubes, ¼" thick
3 tbsp oil
½ tsp jeera
1 piece ginger - grated (1 tbsp)
½ cup ready made tomato puree (100 gm)
½ tsp garam masala, 1½ tsp dhania powder, 1 tsp salt, or to taste
½ tsp red chilli powder
½ tbsp kasoori methi
2 tsp tomato ketchup
½ cup water
½ cup milk
½ cup cream

1. Heat 3 tbsp oil. Add ½ tsp jeera. When it turns golden, add grated ginger. Stir for a minute.
2. Add ½ cup tomato puree. Mix well. Add garam masala, dhania powder, salt and red chilli powder. Cook for 4-5 minutes till tomato puree turns very dry and oil separates. Add kasoori methi and tomato ketchup.
3. Add water. Boil. Simmer on low heat for 4-5 minutes. Reduce heat.
4. Mash 2-3 cubes of paneer and add to the gravy. Add paneer cubes.
5. Keep aside till serving time. (Do not add milk to hot tomato gravy or it might curdle).
6. At serving time, add cold milk and mix very well. Keep on low heat, stirring continuously till it boils. Add cream & stir till just about to boil. Remove from fire. Serve.

Til Mil Aloo Matar

Picture on inside back cover   *Serves 4*

4 small sized potatoes - boiled
3/4 cup boiled or frozen peas
1½ tbsp til (sesame seeds)
3/4 tsp jeera (cumin seeds)
3 tbsp oil
1 large onion - chopped very finely
4-5 cashews - split into halves
10-15 kishmish - soaked in water
1 tsp salt, or to taste
¼ tsp haldi
½ tsp garam masala, ½ tsp red chilli powder, ½ tsp amchoor
2-3 tbsp chopped coriander
2-3 green chillies - whole
2 tsp lemon juice

1. Boil potatoes in salted water until just tender. They should feel soft when a knife is inserted. Do not over cook. (You may also pressure cook the potatoes for a quicker subzi or microwave the potatoes if you wish - 4 potatoes would take about 4 minutes on full power).
2. Peel and cut each potato widthwise into 2 equal halves.
3. Heat oil. Reduce heat. Add til and jeera. Wait till the til (sesame seeds) starts changing colour.
4. Add onions. Cook until onions turn light brown.
5. Add kaju. Stir-fry for a minute. Add kishmish.
6. Add salt, haldi, garam masala, red chilli powder and amchoor. Mix.
7. Add green chillies and fresh coriander. Cook for 1 minute.
8. Add 2-3 tbsp water.
9. Add the potatoes. Stir-fry gently for about 3 minutes on low heat, taking care not to break the potatoes.
10. Finally, add peas. Mix gently. Cook for 2 minutes stirring occasionally. Add lemon juice and mix well. Remove from fire. Serve hot.

Bread Dahi Bada

Serves 4

8 slices of bread, ½ tsp jeera to top
2 cups dahi
salt, pepper, kalanamak, red chilli powder to taste
½ tsp bhuna jeera (roasted cumin seeds)

FILLING
3 tsp very finely cut ginger
2 tbsp finely chopped coriander
6-8 almonds - chopped very finely
½ tsp salt, ¼ tsp red chilli, ¼ tsp garam masala
2 green chillies - deseeded and chopped very finely

BATTER
¼ cup maida, ½ cup water
a pinch of haldi, ¼ tsp red chilli powder

QUICK KHATTI METHI CHUTNEY
1 tbsp amchoor (dried mango powder)
3 tbsp sugar or shakkar (gur)
½ tsp bhuna jeera (roasted cumin seeds) powder
¼ tsp red chilli powder, ¼ tsp salt, ¼ tsp garam masala

1. Mix all the ingredients of the khatti mithi chutney together in a small heavy bottomed pan. Cook on low flame, till all the ingredients dissolve properly and the chutney reaches the right consistency. Keep aside.
2. Prepare a thin batter by mixing all ingredients of the batter together.
3. Mix all ingredients of the filling together - ginger, coriander, almonds, green chillies, salt, garam masala and red chilli powder. Keep aside.
4. Heat oil for deep frying.
5. Cut two rounds with a biscuit cutter or a small katori from each slice of bread. Put some filling on a round piece of bread. Place 1 kishmish on top. Cover with another round and press the two together to join the two pieces of bread. Make 8 such pieces.
6. When the oil is well heated, dip each piece in batter. Press some jeera (cumin seeds) on it & put it in hot oil for frying. The bada swells in oil.

7. Fry one piece at a time. Drain on paper napkins.
8. Beat dahi with ½ tsp bhuna jeera, ¼ tsp kala namak, salt and red chilli powder to taste. Dip the badas in spiced dahi and arrange in a serving dish. Pour the rest of the dahi on top. Sprinkle some bhuna jeera and red chilli powder. Keep in the fridge to let the bread badas get soaked in the dahi for about ½ hour. Serve cold with chutney.

Jeere waale Chaawal

The rice is toasted in oil for 5-7 minutes such that it absorbs all the flavours and each grain remains separate and fluffy. Do not soak the rice but just keep the wet rice in the strainer for some time.

Serves 4

1½ cup uncooked rice - washed, strained and kept in the strainer for 20 minutes
3 tbsp oil, 1 tsp shah jeera (black cumin seeds)
1" stick dalchini (cinnamon), 2 tej patta (bay leaves), 2 laung (cloves)
2 chhoti illaichi (green cardamoms), 3-4 saboot kali mirch (peppercorns)
1 onion - chopped finely, 2 tsp finely chopped ginger
1½ tsp salt, or to taste, juice of ½ lemon (1 tbsp)

1. Heat oil. Reduce heat. Add jeera, dalchini, tej patta, laung, chhoti illaichi and kali mirch. Wait for 1 minute for the spices to turn fragrant.
2. Add onions and ginger. Let onions turn light brown.
3. Add rice. Stir fry gently on low heat for 5-7 minutes till the rice turns brown and toasted. Add 3 cups water, salt and lemon juice. Boil.
4. Cover and cook on a very low fire till done, for about 12-13 minutes.

Shahi Gulabo Kheer

Picture on inside back cover   *Serves 4*

4 cups milk, 1/3 cup sugar
5 tsp cornflour dissolved in ½ cup milk
100 gms paneer (cottage cheese) - grated
2 drops rose essence or 1 tbsp gulab jal, ½ tsp powdered chhoti illaichi
4-5 pista (pistachio) pieces, 4-5 almonds, a few desi rose petals

1. Boil 4 cups milk. Simmer on low flame for 20 minutes.
2. In the meanwhile, boil sugar with 1/3 cup water in a separate pan. Keep on low heat for 5 minutes. Add grated paneer. Cook for 1 minute. Remove from fire and keep aside.
3. Add cornflour paste to the milk of step 1, stirring continuously. Keep stirring for 2 minutes till thick. Add the paneer mixture.
4. Boil. Keep on heat for 1 minute. Remove from fire. Cool. Add essence or gulab jal. Pour in a serving dish. Sprinkle illaichi powder and some shredded pista and almonds. Decorate with rose petals. Serve chilled.

Nita Mehta's **BEST SELLERS (Vegetarian)**

Cakes
& Chocolates

JHATPAT KHAANA

CHAAWAL

BREAKFAST
Vegetarian Special

Food for Children

HANDI TAWA KADHAI

**The art of
BAKING**

MUGHLAI
Vegetarian Khaana

CHINESE
Vegetarian Cuisine

All Time Favourite
SNACKS

South Indian

Vegetarian Dishes

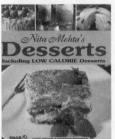